My Aa Book

_____

(name)

The astronaut.

The apple.

The alligator.

The ax.

ABCDEFGHIJKLMNOPQRSTUVWXYZ

The alphabet!

My Bb Book

_____

(name)

See the bee. Buzz!

See the boat.

See the bird.

See the bus.

See the balloon.

My Cc Book

_____

(name)

This is a cup.

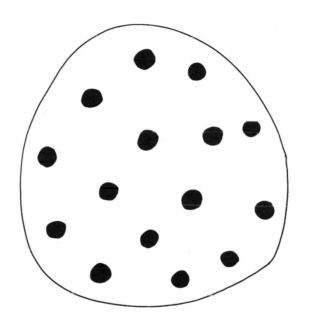

This is a cookie.

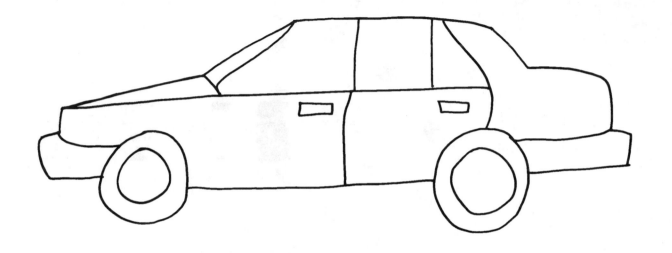

This is a car.

This is a cat.

This is a cupcake. Yum! Yum!

My Dd Book

_____

(name)

A deer can run.

A dog can bark.

A duck can swim.

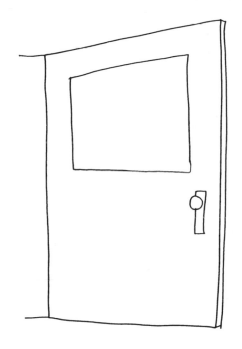

A door can open.

A dinosaur can roar.
Can you?

My Ee Book

_____

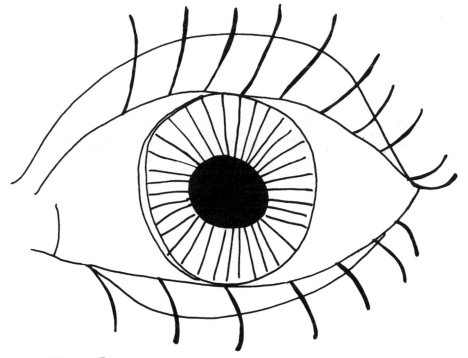

I have an eye.

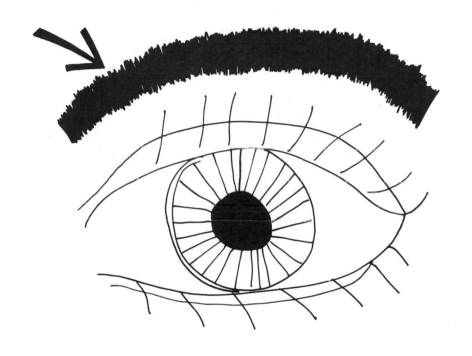

I have an eyebrow.

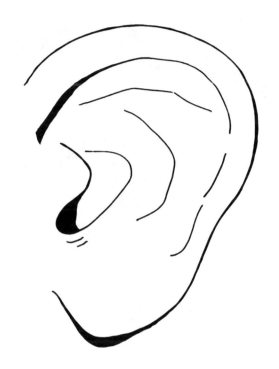

I have an ear.

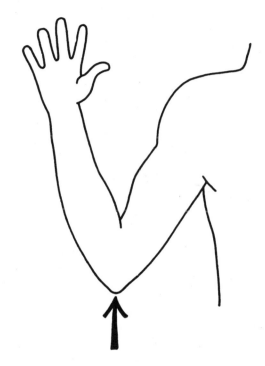

I have an elbow.

I have everything!

My Ff Book

_____

(name)

A fox can run.

A finger can point.

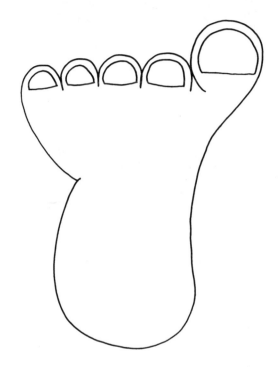

A foot can walk.

A fish can swim.

A frog can jump. So high!

My Gg Book

_____

(name)

I see the goat.

I see the gate.

I see the glasses.

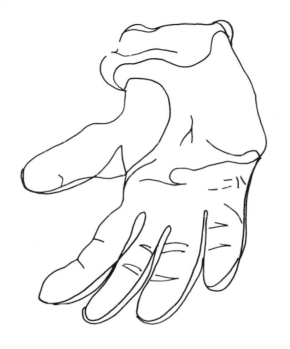

I see the glove.

I see the ghost. Boo!

My Hh Book

_____

(name)

This is a heart.

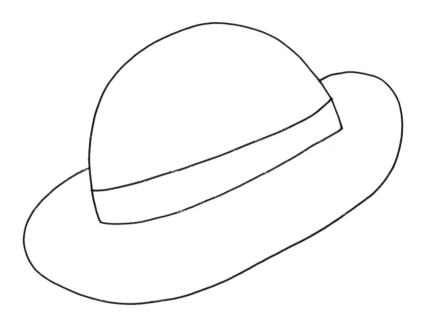

This is a hat.

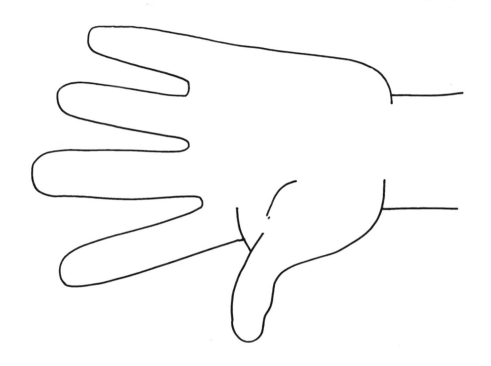

This is a hand.

This is a hen.

This is a house. Mine!

My Ii Book

_____

(name)

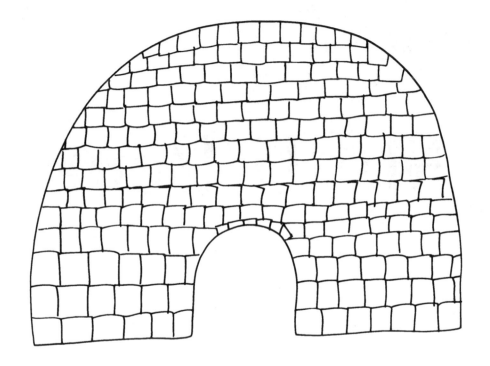

I see the igloo.

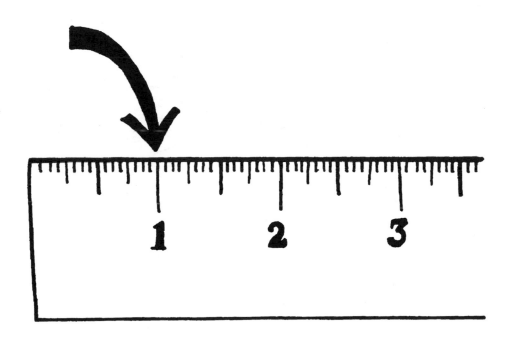

I see the inch.

I see the island.

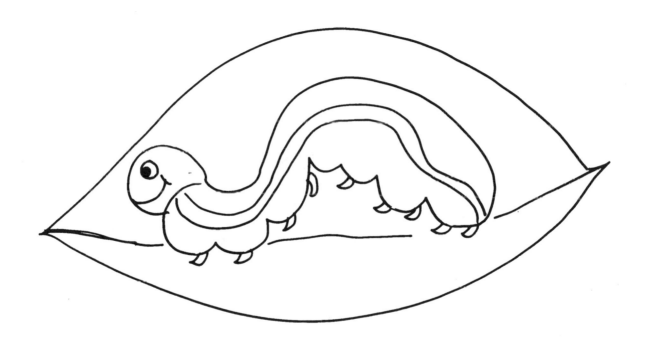

I see the inchworm.

I see the ice cream.
Eat it up!

My Jj Book

_____

(name)

The jeep has wheels.

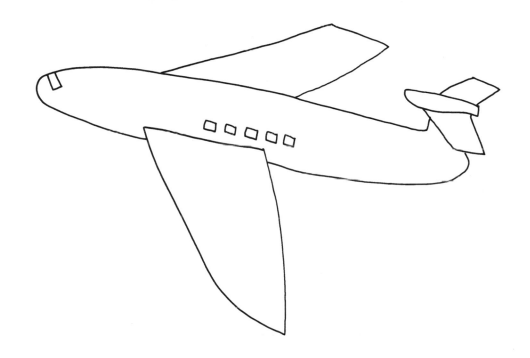

The jet has wings.

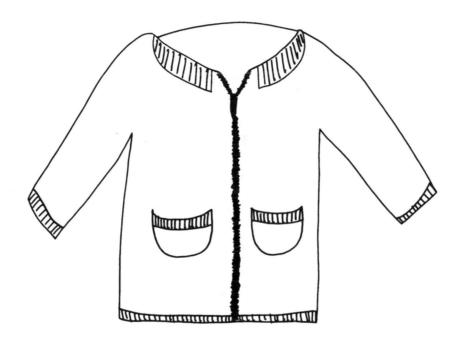

The jacket has pockets.

The jungle has animals.

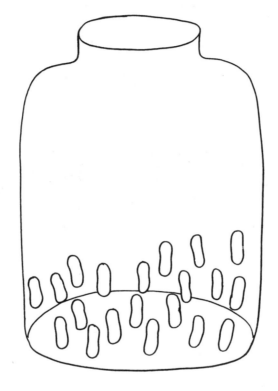

The jar has jelly beans.
How many?

My Kk Book

_____

(name)

Can you see the kangaroo?

Can you see the king?

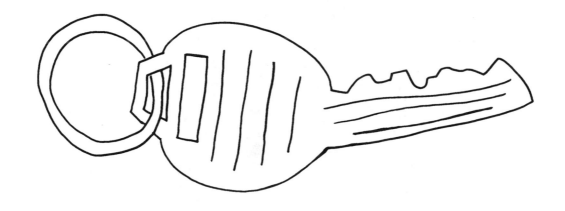

Can you see the key?

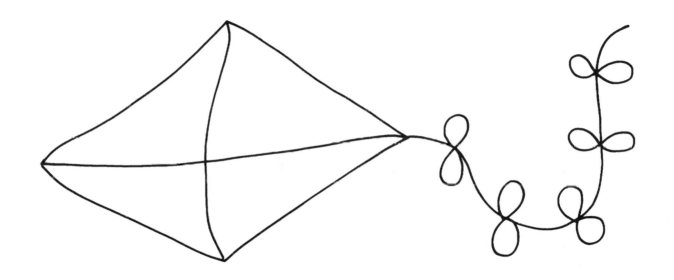

Can you see the kite?

Can you see the kid hiding?
Yes!

My Ll Book

_____

(name)

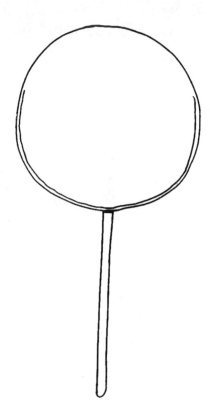

I see the lollipop.

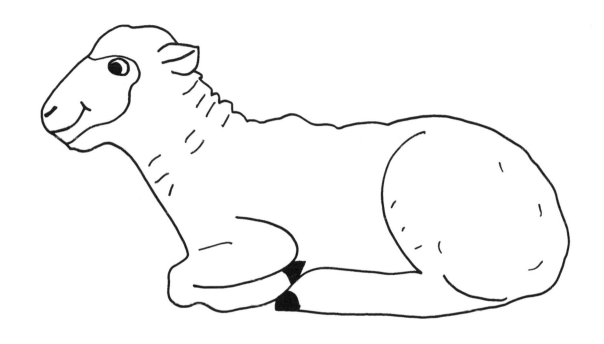

I see the lamb.

I see the lips.

I see the lion.

I see the ladder. Climb it!

My Mm Book

_____

(name)

Look at the monkey.

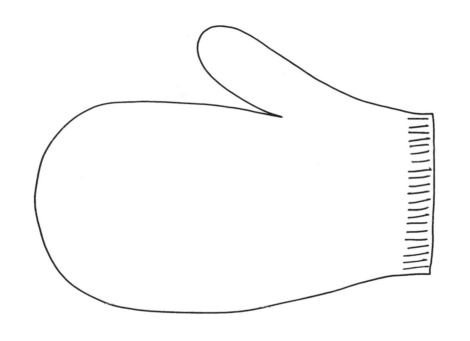

Look at the mitten.

Look at the mouse.

Look at the moon.

Look at the monster. OH NO!

My Nn Book

_____

(name)

The man has a nose.

The giraffe has a long neck.
So long!

The squirrel has a nut.

The girl has a net.

The bird has a nest.

My Oo Book

_____

(name)

Look at the oak tree.

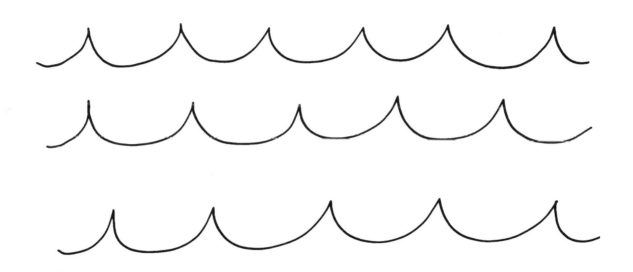

Look at the ocean.

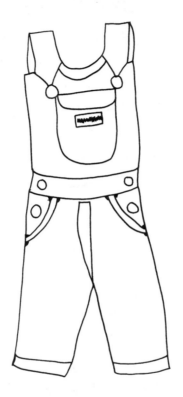

Look at the overalls.

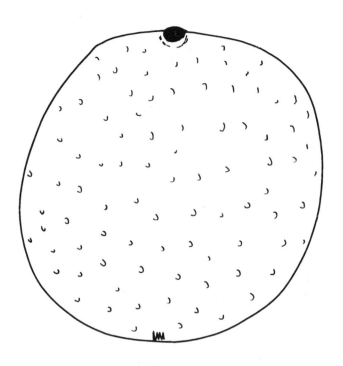

Look at the orange.

Look at the octopus.
Eight legs!

My Pp Book

_____

(name)

The pony can run.

The pig can run.

The penguin can run.

The peacock can run.

The puppy can run to me!

My Qq Book

_____

(name)

Here is a queen.

Here is a quarter.

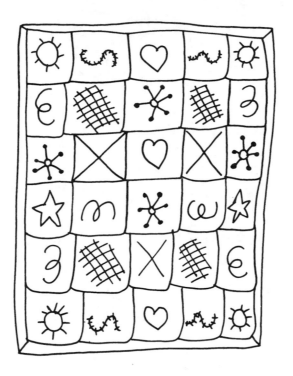

Here is a quilt.

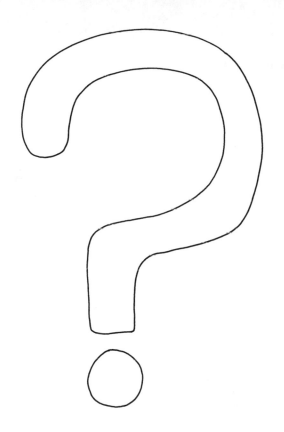

Here is a question mark.
See it?

Here they all are!

My Rr Book

_____

(name)

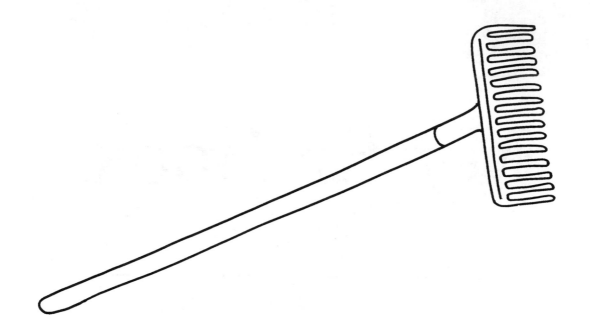

Here is a rake.

Here is a rabbit.

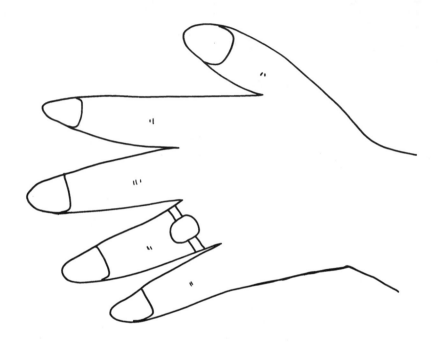

Here is a ring.

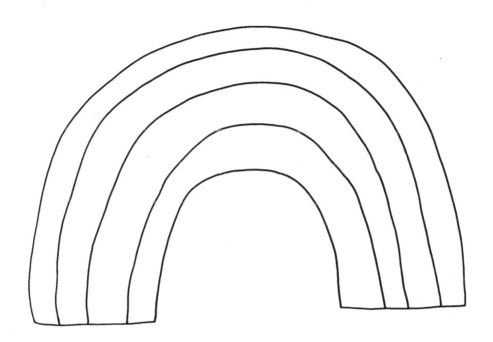

Here is a rainbow.

Here is a rooster.
Cock-a-doodle-doo!

My Ss Book

_____

(name)

This is a sign.

This is a snowman.

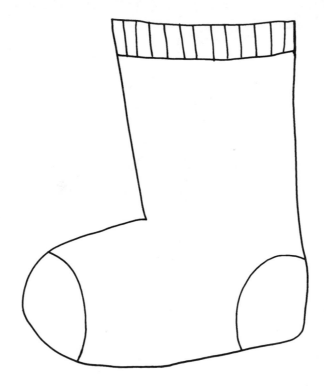

This is a sock.

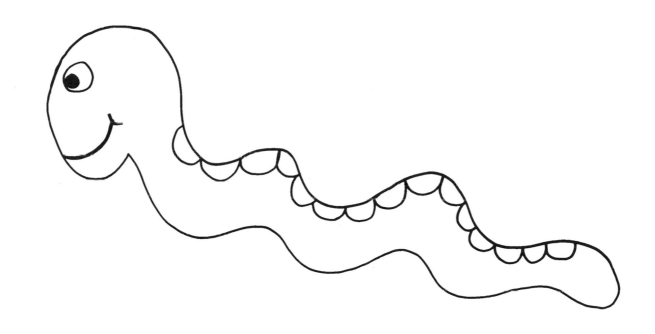

This is a snake.

This is a star. Make a wish!

My Tt Book

_____

(name)

Can you find the turtle?

Can you find the tiger?

Can you find the turkey?

Can you find the teddy bear?

Here they are!

My Uu Book

_____

(name)

See the umpire.

See the umbrella.

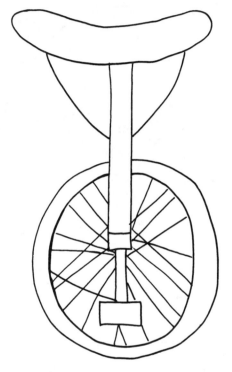

See the unicycle.

See the unicorn.

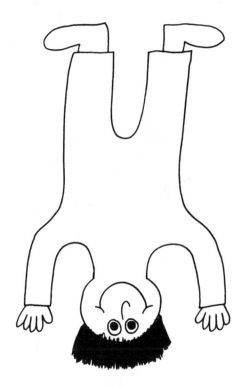

See me. Upside down!

My Vv Book

_____

(name)

Look at the volcano.

Look at the vacuum.

Look at the violin.

Look at the vine.

Look at the valentine.
For you!

My Ww Book

_____

(name)

The watch can tick.

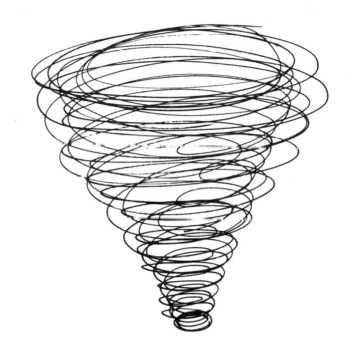

The wind can whirl.

The window can open.

The whale can swim.

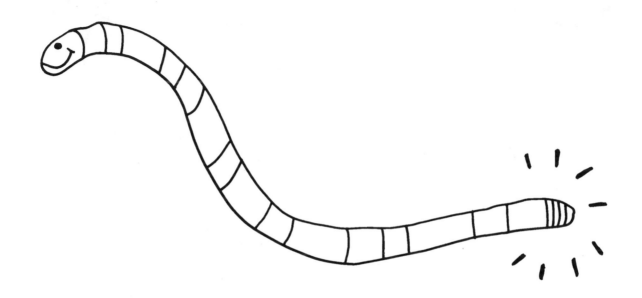

The worm can wiggle.
Wiggle-waggle!

My Xx Book

_____

(name)

I see the head.

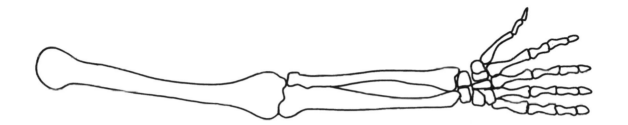

I see the arm.

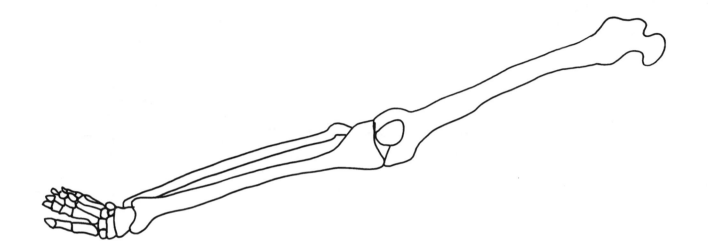

I see the leg.

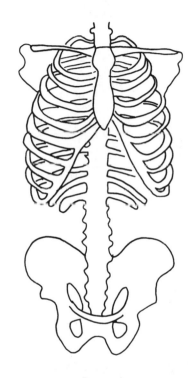

I see the torso.

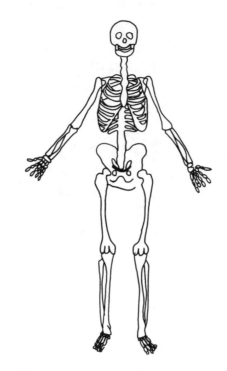

I see the x-ray... of my bones!

My Yy Book

_____

(name)

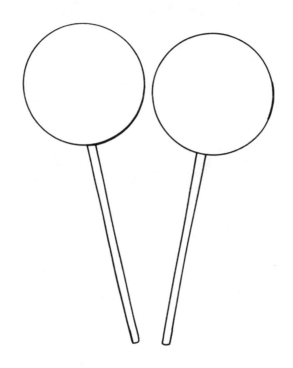

Do you like lollipops? Yes!

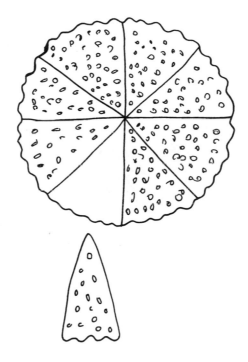

Do you like pizza? Yes!

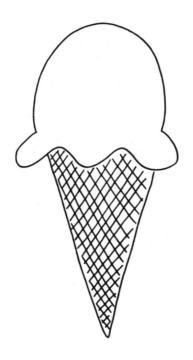

Do you like ice cream? Yes!

Do you like cookies? Yes!

Do you like _____?
Yes! Yum!

My Zz Book

_____

(name)

"Zzz," said the dog.

"Zzz," said the pig.

"Zzz," said the cat.

"Zzz," said the fish.

"Wake up!" I said.
And they did.